FRED BASSET YEARBOOK 2022

An Hachette UK Company
www.hachette.co.uk

Summersdale Publishers Ltd
Part of Octopus Publishing Group Limited
Carmelite House
50 Victoria Embankment
LONDON
EC4Y 0DZ
UK

www.summersdale.com

Printed and bound in the Czech Republic

ISBN: 978-1-80007-003-5

2022

My train of thought!

Substantial discounts on bulk quantities of Summersdale books are available to corporations, professional associations and other organizations.
For details contact general enquiries: telephone: +44 (0) 1243 771107 or email: enquiries@summersdale.com.

They have been clearing out the attic...

HOW ABOUT THIS, DEAR? YEP!

...and off to the boot-fair we go!

It's sad to see my old puppy basket go...

IT'S PERFECT, DEAR!

OH YES — BUBBLES WILL LOVE IT!

YIP

...but I have a feeling that it's going to a good home!